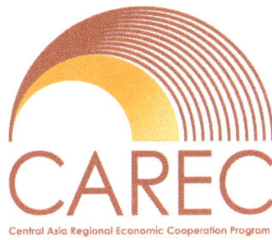

CAREC

Central Asia Regional Economic Cooperation Program

CAREC 2030

CONNECTING THE REGION FOR SHARED AND SUSTAINABLE DEVELOPMENT

October 2017

Printed on recycled paper

CONTENTS

ABBREVIATIONS

ADB	Asian Development Bank
CAREC	Central Asia Regional Economic Cooperation (Program)
CI	CAREC Institute
COP21	21st Conference of the Parties to the United Nations Framework Convention on Climate Change
GDP	gross domestic product
ICT	information and communication technology
MC	ministerial conference
PRC	People's Republic of China
SDG	sustainable development goal
SMEs	small and medium-sized enterprises
SOM	Senior Officials' Meeting
SPS	sanitary and phytosanitary
WTO	World Trade Organization

EXECUTIVE SUMMARY

Strategic Directions

CAREC 2030 provides the new long-term strategic framework for the Central Asia Regional Economic Cooperation (CAREC) Program leading to 2030. It is inspired by a mission to create an open and inclusive regional cooperation platform that connects people, policies, and projects for shared and sustainable development.

CAREC 2030 builds on the solid foundation of progress made under CAREC 2020, the strategy that has guided CAREC's activities since 2011. The strategy is now being revisited to ensure CAREC's relevance in the fast-changing development landscape of member countries in the region, and in view of the emerging challenges to globalization posed by the stalemate in progressing global trade deals and rising protectionism in various parts of the world. The need and usefulness of regional approaches to cooperation and integration has redoubled in these circumstances.

CAREC 2030 aligns its activities with national strategies and development plans and with the new international development agenda embodied in the sustainable development goals (SDGs) and the 21st Conference of the Parties to the United Nations Framework Convention on Climate Change (COP21) global climate agreement. It will support regional actions that must complement national efforts to successfully address the SDGs and climate change. *CAREC 2030* will embrace such areas as resilient infrastructure development, natural capital and the environment, sustainable urbanization, and inclusive social development. It will also devise sustainable financing plans to support these ambitious goals.

To align with national and international goals and to increase its relevance and effectiveness, CAREC's operations will be both deepened in the existing priority areas of transport, energy, and trade; and scaled up to include new areas. Besides project investments, *CAREC 2030* will promote policy dialogue among members and development partners, and deliver and disseminate quality knowledge services. The CAREC Institute will be central to providing knowledge solutions. CAREC's reputation as a neutral, honest broker will help it catalyze technically sound and balanced development solutions based on best practice.

Moreover, *CAREC 2030* will promote business-to-business contacts across members. Civil society will be strengthened through promoting people-to-people contacts across borders.

The CAREC platform will welcome existing and new development partners. Partners will be encouraged to lead dialogue and operations in priority areas using the CAREC platform.

Operational Priorities

CAREC 2030 envisages focus on five operational clusters going forward: (i) economic and financial stability; (ii) trade, tourism, and economic corridors; (iii) infrastructure and economic connectivity; (iv) agriculture and water; and (v) human development. Integrating the use of information and communication technology (ICT) across the spectrum of CAREC operations will be a cross-cutting priority.

(i) For economic and financial stability, CAREC will promote policy dialogue and regional learning on macroeconomic policy coordination, including forging appropriate countercyclical policy responses at the regional level during periods of economic crisis. By setting up a forum to exchange experiences, CAREC will support national banking and capital market regulators in data exchange, intelligence, and implement agreed common practices.

(ii) For trade, CAREC will help assess the shifting landscape of global and regional trade, and the potential of moving toward free trade agreements in the region, with a focus on trade in services, including tourism. It will assist members with the range of World Trade Organization (WTO)-related commitments, with respect to trade facilitation and policy. Support for national single windows, improved border crossing points, and customs harmonization will be provided. Economic corridor development and related urbanization strategies will be facilitated.

(iii) For regional infrastructure development, investments in railways and logistics will be stepped-up, commercial capabilities strengthened, and regulatory frameworks modernized. Aviation priorities will address international aviation agreements, including open skies, and knowledge and capacity consistent with international standards. Priority will be maintained on road safety and road asset management. *CAREC 2030* will support technology leapfrogging in the use of clean and renewable energy, and promote energy efficiency, besides promoting energy trade.

(iv) For agriculture, support for sanitary and phytosanitary measures will help CAREC countries integrate into global agricultural value chains. Support can also be considered for transboundary animal disease control. CAREC will use its honest broker role to promote dialogue on water management issues. Irrigation, improved management of rivers to reduce flood risk, and addressing water contamination are some "early harvest" areas for support. Assistance could be provided in basin water management, particularly in transboundary areas.

(v) For human development, CAREC will help develop a regional labor market information system focusing on skills needs, regional job search and placement, and cross-border higher education and technical training offerings. CAREC will help address pandemic risks and control of communicable diseases, and prevention and treatments for noncommunicable diseases.

Institutional Arrangements

A renewed institutional framework will be required to implement *CAREC 2030*, guided by strong country and development partner ownership and strengthened engagement with the private sector and civil society. The Ministerial Conference will function as a strategy-setting and policy body, and exercise accountability over the results of the CAREC Program. The Senior Officials' Meeting will monitor overall operational progress and consider complex multisector projects.

Sector committees will be further strengthened with full operational authorities, and flexible operating arrangements will be introduced, supported by expert groups. Focus group discussions will be required to set agendas for CAREC's new operational priorities.

Resources

Greater financial and other resources will be indispensable to support *CAREC 2030*. Development partners will need to scale up their financial and technical support for CAREC projects and activities. As public sector financing alone cannot meet the large investment requirements, *CAREC 2030* will help members obtain private sector financing by deploying public funds for de-risking and leveraging private investments. Member countries may consider more contributions to support and sustain the CAREC Program and its activities.

Results

A program results framework will monitor CAREC's progress, showing the results chain that leads from program interventions to the expected outputs and the targeted outcomes in each operational cluster. The CAREC Secretariat will support development of cluster-specific results frameworks that will include concrete indicators, baseline data, and data sources. An online system of tracking and updating progress on these indicators with regular intervals will be established.

I INTRODUCTION

1. The CAREC Program,[1] now 16 years in operation, has recorded impressive achievements in regional economic cooperation, particularly in the four priority areas of transport, energy, trade facilitation, and trade policy. Since 2001, investments in member countries under CAREC have amounted to more than $30 billion.[2] Six international development institutions participate,[3] buttressing a robust program of project investments and knowledge products (see Appendix).

2. CAREC operations have been guided by the strategic framework outlined in CAREC 2020,[4] that covers the period 2011–2020. The vision articulated in the strategic framework is one of *Good Neighbors, Good Partners, and Good Prospects. CAREC 2020* envisages development through cooperation, leading to accelerated growth and shared prosperity, based upon trade expansion and improved competitiveness. To support these objectives, CAREC has been promoting cooperation in the four priority areas as well as economic corridors development, "second-tier" areas,[5] and the CAREC Institute.

3. CAREC 2020 notes that the strategic framework is expected to undergo refinement during the strategy period. A Midterm Review of CAREC 2020, completed in 2016, acknowledged the significant progress in addressing the agenda set out in CAREC 2020. It also recognized the need to review the strategic coherence and the relevance of CAREC. This was with the backdrop of the unexpected and significant changes in the international economic environment that had a major impact on several CAREC countries. Development priorities of CAREC countries have been also shifting. The Midterm Review thus recommended:

- completing the CAREC 2020 agenda, sharpening the focus on expanding trade and competitiveness of its members;

- revisiting CAREC's objectives to ensure these are strategically coherent, aimed at serving the highest development priorities;

- broadening the CAREC agenda beyond energy and transport through consultations with members with possible new areas being private sector development, information and communication technology (ICT), agriculture, food security, education, health, and tourism; and

- preparing a new long-term strategy for CAREC to include an updated partnership structure reflecting growing regional and financial initiatives among its members, and the emergence of new financial institutions.

4. *CAREC 2030* was prepared in a thoroughly consultative and participatory manner. During the first half of 2017, consultations were conducted in all CAREC member countries, involving more than 350 government officials, multilateral and bilateral development partners, think tanks, academia, the private sector, and business associations. The valuable guidance and inputs received through these consultations are reflected in this strategy paper.

---

[1] The Central Asia Regional Economic Cooperation Program has a membership of 11 states, with the original eight members being Afghanistan, Azerbaijan, People's Republic of China (Xinjiang joined in 1997; Inner Mongolia in 2008), Kazakhstan, the Kyrgyz Republic, Mongolia, Tajikistan, and Uzbekistan. Pakistan and Turkmenistan joined in 2010; Georgia in 2016.

[2] As of end September 2017, investments in member countries under CAREC amounted to $30.5 billion, covering 182 projects.

[3] Asian Development Bank, European Bank for Reconstruction and Development, International Monetary Fund, Islamic Development Bank, United Nations Development Programme, and the World Bank Group.

[4] ADB. 2012. *CAREC 2020: A Strategic Framework for the CAREC Program.* Manila.

[5] As explained in CAREC 2020, the second-tier areas could cover control of communicable diseases, agriculture, disaster risk management, and climate change adaptation and mitigation, in the context of addressing social impacts of trade expansion and improved competitiveness.

RATIONALE FOR
CAREC 2030

CAREC is repositioning itself against the backdrop of a fast-changing global and regional landscape

5. The CAREC strategy needs to be updated because of several national, regional, and global developments that may impact CAREC's relevance and effectiveness going forward. *CAREC 2030* recognizes the following important developments.

• *Growth and macroeconomic context in CAREC countries*

6. Since 2001, CAREC's investments have contributed to sustained economic growth in the region. The CAREC region's gross domestic product (GDP) grew at an average rate of about 9% per year during 2003–2007. The 2007–2008 global economic and financial crisis interrupted this growth significantly and the adverse impacts of the crisis have lingered. During 2012–2016, the average annual growth rate nearly halved to 4.7%.[6]

7. The dive in commodity prices beginning in 2014 further damaged the balance sheets of hydrocarbon-exporting countries, and the resulting recession dampened prospects of migrant labor and reduced the flow of remittances to labor exporting countries. CAREC countries faced urgent economic problems, including fiscal pressures, devaluing currencies, rising current account deficits, and lowered foreign reserves that led to stagnating economic activity, higher unemployment, and a rollback of structural and sector reforms. On top of this, the economic slowdown of the major trading partners led to shrinking markets for exports originating in CAREC countries. Against this backdrop, *CAREC 2030* can provide a regional forum to develop common approaches, and learn from regional experience in sustaining economic growth and in the application of countercyclical policies to mitigate economic downturns.

• *The global and regional trade environment*

8. Historically, the world trade volume has grown 1.5 times faster than world GDP. However, since 2012, the trade volume barely kept pace with growth. More recently, a recovery is underway with the global trade volume growing by 4.2% year-on-year in the first quarter of 2017.[7] In the CAREC region, there was an even sharper decline in trade, from a trade to GDP ratio of 1.8 in 2003–2007 to below 1.0 since 2013.[8] Early signs of recovery in the region are now seen, with a 2.3% growth in trade in 2016.

9. The waning pace of trade liberalization and the rise of protectionist sentiments could continue to affect global trade patterns. At the same time, the failure to agree on global trade

---

[6] United Nations Congress on Trade and Development (UNCTAD) Statistics. Data for PRC not included in the calculations. http://unctadstat.unctad.org/wds/ReportFolders/reportFolders.aspx?sCS_ChosenLang=en

[7] WTO Short-Term Trade Statistics. 2017 https://www.wto.org/english/res_e/statis_e/short_term_stats_e.htm

[8] Ibid.

[9] The Doha Round, officially launched in November 2001 at the WTO's fourth ministerial conference in Doha, Qatar, is the latest trade-negotiation round among the WTO membership. It aimed to achieve a major reform of the international trading system through lowered trade barriers and revised trade rules.

deals exemplified in the stalemate in the WTO post-Doha rounds [9] and the lack of progress on the Trans-Pacific Partnership agreement may provide an opportunity to seek greater progress in regional trade agreements. *CAREC 2030* will consider these developments to reposition itself as a catalyst for trade expansion and economic diversification in the region.

- *Emerging regional players*

10. Multilateral and bilateral mechanisms for regional economic cooperation have multiplied over time. The scope for establishing constructive regional partnerships has increased, and so have the risks posed by lack of coordination and overlapping mandates. This underscores the need for CAREC to carefully assess emerging opportunities of partnerships and strengthen coordination with such regional frameworks and institutions to effectively respond to the region's contemporary challenges.

- *New development goals*

11. All CAREC countries are signatories to the 2030 global development agenda, including the sustainable development goals (SDGs) and the Paris agreement reached at the 21st Conference of Parties of UN Framework Convention on Climate Change (COP21). CAREC needs to consider the implications of the international development goals and the expectations from member countries for support from regional cooperation programs to achieve these goals.

DRIVING PRINCIPLES OF *CAREC 2030*

12. Five driving principles guided the preparation and priority-setting for *CAREC 2030*. These include the following:

- *Aligning with national strategies and supporting SDGs and COP21*

13. First, *CAREC 2030* needs to be aligned with national strategies to create greater national ownership and will support country-level goals and objectives (see Box). It is also closely connected with the SDGs and the COP21 climate agreement, a task facilitated by several national strategies developed in the backdrop of these international development goals.

14. *CAREC 2030* will promote regional approaches that complement national actions to best achieve the international development goals, focusing on those where externalities prevail or spillover effects are strong. CAREC will provide technical solutions in support of plans, new avenues for financing, and promote development effectiveness through coordinated approaches. Considerations of sustainability and climate resilience will cut across all CAREC investments.

- *Expanding operational priorities selectively*

15. Second, CAREC's operational priorities need to be expanded in a carefully calibrated manner to align with national strategies and international goals, meet the expectations of member countries, and strengthen CAREC's relevance going forward. This expansion will be two-pronged. First, building on its comparative advantages and learning from its experience,

CAREC will deepen and scale up operations in its traditional areas of transport, energy, trade, and economic corridor development to boost growth. And, second, CAREC will support operations in selective new areas identified as additional priorities (see Chapter V for details on *CAREC 2030*'s operational priorities).

16. Deepening of CAREC's support in existing areas and entry into new areas will be gradual and incremental; it will be tailored to the resources and capabilities made available by all member countries and development partners, and it will be backed by sound institutional arrangements and capacity development to ensure effective and timely execution of operations.

17. The enlarged scope of the program will afford new opportunities for all CAREC's development partners, both existing and new, to provide support and expertise and lead operations in areas of their respective comparative advantage. It will also provide avenues for capitalizing on linkages and synergies between sectors, such as those that exist between the water, agriculture, and energy sectors.

18. Integrating the use of ICT across the spectrum of CAREC operations is a priority to raise the quality of public services and support private sector growth. CAREC countries still need to bridge the digital divide, which requires ICT investments and knowledge services to improve accessibility and efficiency in public services, upgrade productivity, enable smoother people-to-people contacts and support integration in regional and global value chains. The trans-

CAREC will deepen support in existing sectors and selectively expand into new areas to align with national strategies and international development goals

Eurasian information super-highway (TASIM) project represents an example of on-going efforts to promote digital connectivity within the region and beyond.

- *Deepening policy dialogue based on CAREC's standing and ability to deliver quality knowledge services.*

19.   Third, CAREC's 16-year history of operations, its convening power, and its role as a neutral honest broker lend it credibility in moderating regional discussions and negotiations. Its informal structure facilitates policy dialogue, especially on complex and sensitive development issues. These strengths will be preserved and emphasized under *CAREC 2030* as the program deepens its footprint in existing areas and expands into new areas requiring intensive inter-country dialogue.

20. Development dialogues facilitated by CAREC will be grounded in knowledge work member countries and development partners undertake, and coordinated with other knowledge providers to multiply the range of available knowledge solutions, and minimize duplication and overlap.

21.   The CAREC Institute (CI) will be central to providing knowledge solutions. The CI will play a key role in developing knowledge and analytical underpinnings for policy dialogue at the CAREC's Ministerial Conference (MC), Senior Officials' Meeting (SOM), and sector coordinating committees. By building formal links with academia and think tanks in the region, the CI will make best use of local knowledge. The CI will be a repository of knowledge, build international best practices drawn from the available global knowledge base, and provide cutting-edge capacity building and training services to help uplift policy development, governance, and service standards across member countries.

CAREC will strengthen engagement with all stakeholders through policy dialogue, and project incubation and implementation

- *Integrating the role of the private sector and civil society*

22. Fourth, private sector's participation and investment in the CAREC region to promote economic stability, sustain growth, and create jobs is crucial and needs to be promoted. In the CAREC context, the private sector can take a lead role in transforming transport corridors into economic corridors, expanding trade and investment, supporting agricultural value chains, developing cross-border tourism, and spearheading regional education and health initiatives. Thus, *CAREC 2030* will promote business-to-business contacts among member countries for embedding regional cooperation in national plans and priorities. Mutually beneficial regional opportunities will be promoted through business and investment forums, bringing the public and private sectors together, and strengthening linkages between them.

23. Without private sector financing, the large investment requirements of the CAREC region cannot be met. The SDGs themselves require financing in amounts that significantly exceed volumes of official development assistance; consideration must be given to tapping pools of domestic and international private capital.[10] *CAREC 2030* will help member countries leverage private sector financing solutions by deploying public funds for de-risking and leveraging up private investments. Due attention needs to be paid to creating incentive structures, institutions, and the public interface to attract such investments.

24. *CAREC 2030* will strengthen engagement with civil society to seek its support in promoting people-to-people contacts, including among border communities with strong traditional ties across countries. Student exchange programs,

---

[10]   Multilateral development banks have noted that "achieving the SDGs will require moving from billions to trillions in resource flows. Such a paradigm shift calls for a wide-ranging financing framework capable of channeling resources and investments of all kinds—public and private, national and global." African Development Bank et al. 2016. *From Billions to Trillions: Transforming Development Finance.* Washington, DC.

medical patients' visits to tertiary health care facilities in neighboring countries, and opening of bilateral and regional tourism opportunities can help bring people together and confer direct and tangible benefits to cross-border populations at large. More attention will be paid to gender equality as a cross-cutting issue in the above areas.

- *Building an open, inclusive CAREC platform*

25. Finally, CAREC should become an open and inclusive platform to maximize its development partners' resources and expertise to support regional cooperation. To this end, the CAREC platform will welcome both existing and new international development partners to contribute to the program on an equal footing. Development partners will be encouraged to lead dialogue and operations in *CAREC 2030*'s priority areas and channel their support using the CAREC platform.

26. CAREC will seek to strengthen coordination with other international and regional cooperation mechanisms active in the region including the Belt and Road Initiative, Shanghai Cooperation Organization and Economic Cooperation Organization. In addition, CAREC will recognize the importance of economic ties with non-CAREC neighboring countries and will coordinate activities with relevant entities, especially in the commercial and academic spheres.

27. A robust communications strategy will be developed to demonstrate CAREC's drive for transparency and sharing of information, as well as enhancing public awareness of its role in member countries and beyond. Stronger publicity from governments, greater visibility and recognition in the development world, and a higher public profile would add to CAREC's legitimacy and aid its effectiveness.

Box: Aligning *CAREC 2030* to National Strategies

In the member countries' national development strategies, currently being pursued or being designed, several CAREC-supported themes emerge strongly. All development strategies place economic growth and job creation at their center, with a focus on a sound macroeconomic framework and financial sector stability. Kazakhstan's strategy is directed at economic diversification. The Afghanistan *National Peace and Development Framework* looks for improvements in bank regulation and financial sector inclusion; the Pakistan *Vision-2025* aims at financial deepening. Three other strategies—of Azerbaijan, the Kyrgyz Republic, and Uzbekistan—look for regional approaches to contain economic and exchange rate volatility, aim at steadiness in monetary policies, and strengthening of the financial sector. Azerbaijan and Mongolia place banking sector and capital market reforms as the essential part of their medium-term strategies. Georgia is also implementing broad-based reforms, including capital market and pension reforms. The development strategy of Xinjiang (PRC), places emphasis on financial inclusion. Fiscal and monetary policy liberalization and the development of insurance markets are late-stage elements in Turkmenistan's reform strategy to 2030. Countries are looking to stabilize cross-country capital flows and to develop capital markets.

Transport features prominently, especially in the context of regional corridors, but also in the areas of improving asset management, institutions, and financing in Afghanistan, Pakistan, and the Central Asian countries. All countries recognize in their national development strategies the critical importance of improved water resource management (Pakistan), improved water storage (Afghanistan, Pakistan, and Uzbekistan), and cooperation in optimizing water-energy linkages. Agriculture plays a prominent role in the development strategies of Afghanistan, Kazakhstan, the Kyrgyz Republic, and Uzbekistan, with an emphasis on efficient water use.

Member countries are attempting to raise energy efficiency—Kazakhstan, Pakistan, Tajikistan, and Uzbekistan, in particular—while pursuing their climate-change national contributions. A rise in electricity supply will require a much larger share of clean energy (especially in Kazakhstan, Pakistan, and Uzbekistan), as their national strategies recognize. The shift to hydrogeneration and the growing role of public–private partnerships is discussed in Afghanistan's strategy; Mongolia's strategy even discusses carbon sequestration possibilities. Clean energy is prominent in the strategy of Georgia, Inner Mongolia (PRC), and Turkmenistan. Energy trade is given great importance in the strategies of many CAREC members, and national strategies emphasize the role regional cooperation must play for trade to take place smoothly.

Trade is central in almost all national development strategies, with members aspiring to fulfill WTO obligations (or harmonize with them in the case of some non-WTO members). Trade facilitation improvements are sought through single window operations and ICT-assisted information flows. Tourism is the subject of ambitious development plans stretching to 2025 in Azerbaijan and Georgia, and in Mongolia, Tajikistan, and Uzbekistan; ICT-fueled tourism growth is also key in the Almaty–Bishkek economic corridor.

In the above areas, national strategies place importance on the role of the private sector, on regulatory systems that provide incentives to private investments, on making public–private partnerships work better, and on tapping emerging new sources of financing. Moreover, both Azerbaijan and Uzbekistan seek to stimulate privatizations and improve the business environment, not least in logistics and trade.

Regional cooperation in health is found in several national strategies, particularly in cross-border control of diseases, preparing for pandemics, and seeking common solutions in, for example, noncommunicable diseases. Kazakhstan (Astana) hosts the Global Disease Detection Center. Georgia's *Four Point Plan* (2016) includes education reform as one of the most important priorities, in the belief that an insufficiently qualified labor force is the biggest obstacle to doing business. Education reforms center on setting curriculum standards, adopting a new teacher policy framework, adult learning, introducing vocational training, and adopting a dual work-based learning approach.

Source: CAREC Secretariat.

CAREC 2030 MISSION STATEMENT

28. *CAREC 2030* will retain the overarching CAREC vision of *Good Neighbors, Good Partners, and Good Prospects*. To achieve this vision, the proposed mission statement of *CAREC 2030* is

A Regional Cooperation Platform to Connect People, Policies, and Projects for Shared and Sustainable Development

29. The mission statement signifies important directional changes in CAREC's approach going forward. First, it envisages CAREC as an open and inclusive "platform" where member countries and development partners come together to plan regional cooperation initiatives. As stated in para. 25, in addition to the six existing official

development partners, the new CAREC will be open to new partners willing to contribute to its mission and objectives.

30. Second, the mission statement cements the intent for CAREC to pursue a *"projects++" approach*. Under this approach, CAREC's historical emphasis on regional projects will be complemented with a framework for policy dialogue and knowledge cooperation on the one hand, and promoting people-to-people contacts on the other, as part of a holistic and encompassing strategy to deepen regional integration.

31. And, third, the quest for shared and sustainable development in the mission statement shows the resolve to align closely with member countries' national strategies, and with the SDGs and COP21 climate agreement, that also pursue the same objectives.

V RENEWING CAREC'S OPERATIONAL FRAMEWORK

32. CAREC 2030 prioritizes five operational clusters, encompassing existing and proposed areas. In addition, it supports the use of ICT to promote productivity and efficiency gains in all operational clusters.

33. Three criteria were used in selecting the operational clusters and their constituent sectors. First, the clusters show high returns to regional approaches, transcending the returns to individual country efforts. Second, the clusters are aligned with the priorities of national development strategies and the international development goals. And, third, CAREC's development partners enjoy strong comparative advantages in these clusters, or can build up their expertise rapidly to support member countries in these.

A. Economic and Financial Stability Cluster

i. Macroeconomic Policy Coordination

34. With the region's susceptibility to external economic shocks, CAREC will help support stable macroeconomic conditions and sound banking systems and capital markets as vital ingredients for economic growth and poverty reduction. CAREC will assist with policy dialogue and regional learning to design and implement appropriate countercyclical policy responses in periods of economic downturns. The MC could lead this dialogue. CAREC will particularly focus its expertise to illustrate sector linkages with macroeconomic performance; for example, the impact of energy pricing reforms on fiscal balance and economic stability in member countries.

35. To facilitate regional dialogue and minimize negative spillover effects under the CAREC umbrella, development partners will work together to support consistency of policy approaches in member countries. At a future stage, such cooperation dialogue could evolve into mutually supportive arrangements to deal with external shocks; for example, countries benefiting from an oil price rise could find ways of cushioning the effects on those adversely affected to support demand, not least for their non-oil exports. Another example could be arrangements on currency swaps between central banks based on lessons learned from the Chiang Mai Initiative.[11]

36. CAREC development partners can continue to provide medium-term lending to countries affected by economic shocks and those needing financing for economic adjustment, while promoting cross-country coordination and learning to improve the designs of subsequent interventions.

---

[11] Multilateral currency swap arrangement among the 10 members of the Association of Southeast Asian Nations, PRC, Japan, and Republic of Korea.

ii.   Promoting Financial Stability

37. Strengthening financial infrastructure and access to finance are high priorities across the CAREC membership. Growing cross-border capital flows strengthen financial integration, as does better-coordinated banking sector regulation and disclosure requirements, ease in use of collateral for loans, and other measures to raise credit-worthiness. Improving and standardizing banking supervision and enabling capital market reforms are also critical to forging closer financial cooperation among CAREC countries.

38. By setting up a forum to exchange experience and lessons, *CAREC 2030* will support national banking and capital market regulators' needs to exchange data, intelligence, and develop common practices to international standards, including Basel II and III. Such a forum could also deliberate on common frameworks in banking supervision, the avoidance of contagion effects, and measures to deal with impediments to cross-border transactions.

39. The creation of market institutions, such as the Astana International Financial Center, could focus on serving regional clients. Likewise, Pakistan's experience with capital market development and regulatory strengthening could offer useful lessons for deepening market structures in other CAREC countries. CAREC development partners can encourage reforms in capital markets development, corporate governance, risk management, and local bond and stock market development, leading to eventual cross-listing of securities. Such reforms will require establishing robust ICT systems.

40. In addition, three region-wide proposals for deepening of financial markets merit consideration. First, the development of trade finance and the possible establishment of a multilateral trade credit and investment guarantee agency to cover CAREC members.[12] Second, promoting the use of local currencies for regional trade and banking operations across the membership. And, third, bolstering small and medium-sized enterprises (SMEs) financing, which is a common constraint in most member countries, and where cross-country learning could be useful to adopt effective financing models.

iii.   Strengthening the Investment Climate

41. Stronger macroeconomic and financial stability will lead to an improvement in the outlook for investment in CAREC countries. Nearly all member countries, however, perform poorly on investment climate indicators at present.[13] *CAREC 2030* will promote reforms to attract greater private sector investment, including cross-border investment in member countries. Efforts will focus on reducing investor transaction costs, redressing incoherent or inaccurate investment policies and regulations, promoting business linkages between multinationals and domestics SMEs, and supporting capital markets development. To promote economic diversification, CAREC will support cross-border private sector investments in agriculture, agribusiness development and manufacturing, tourism, education, health, and other service sectors.

B.   Trade, Tourism, and Economic Corridors Cluster

i.   Trade

42. CAREC facilitated trade openness by preparing member countries for WTO membership, and helping them with post-accession needs; by expanding trade in services; and by addressing nontariff barriers. CAREC's trade facilitation agenda recorded successes with both knowledge and institution building: for knowledge building, international best practices were introduced in border management, logistics, sanitary and phytosanitary measures (SPS); in institution building, customs and freight forwarding cooperation institutions were formed and capacity built up. Pilot projects on customs control, prearrival data exchange, and regional transit are under implementation.

43. Going forward, CAREC will assess the shifting landscape of global and regional trade paradigms,

> **CAREC will support macroeconomic and financial stability for stronger economic resilience and an improved investment climate**

---

[12]   This agency will foster inter- and intra-regional trade and investment by providing credit and investment insurance and guarantees, as well as other risk mitigation instruments and financial services. Such instruments and services will help increase foreign direct investment and improve access to trade finance in CAREC countries.

[13]   Georgia is a notable exception.

and the potential of moving toward free trade agreements in the region. Opportunities for the CAREC countries in the context of trade treaties[14] under discussion need to be understood and taken advantage of. CAREC will produce analyses for its members, outlining new opportunities, and help devise trade promotion strategies.

44. A continued focus on trade in services, particularly in e-commerce, and cross-border labor placements can yield rich dividends. Prerequisites for success are investments in backbone services such as telecommunications or financial services, and freer movement of labor.

45. A special task for *CAREC 2030* is to help members with obligations on post WTO-accession commitments, embracing difficult areas of trade adjustment where international agreements come into effect, such as the agreement on technical barriers to trade, the agreement on the application of SPS measures, and the trade facilitation agreement,[15] all of them under the WTO's aegis. *CAREC 2030* will continue to support accession process for member countries that are not WTO members.

46. Regional cooperation in the implementation of the WTO–Trade Facilitation Agreement will be promoted through both knowledge and project solutions. Efforts on customs and integrated trade facilitation will be deepened through (i) establishment of national single windows, (ii) improvement of border crossing points, (iii) customs simplification and harmonization, including alignment with the Revised Kyoto Convention;[16] (iv) establishment of a regional transit regime; and (v) development of logistics centers. Furthermore, the CAREC advanced transit system will be scaled up, the information common exchange across customs will be extended to all members and cover all trade and transit transactions, and new border service improvements projects will be undertaken.

Regional cooperation will benefit from enhanced trade openness, joint tourism initiatives, and economic corridor development

ii.   Tourism

47. Trade in one category of services—tourism—enjoys high potential among the CAREC membership. Sustainable tourism, including community-based and urban tourism, and nature and ecotourism (often cross-boundary) provide particularly important opportunities given the region's rich natural endowments. With the member countries' binding cultural ties and their arresting natural attributes, such as areas and routes rich in history or nature parks, and mountains and forests that traverse national boundaries, CAREC will promote a regional approach to tourism development to maximize economic opportunities and to safeguard ecosystems. Common services, such as mountain rescue services, tour guides, and hiking can be developed to realize economies of scale.

48. CAREC can support the region's large untapped tourism potential through advertising and branding, investing in tourism services and critical infrastructure, jointly developing tourist products, and advocating harmonization and relaxation of visa regimes.

iii.   Economic Corridors Support Urbanization

49. Economic corridors exploit the strong growth effects of agglomeration that accompanies urbanization; these effects are amplified if resilient infrastructure linkages exist and conditions are propitious for private sector investments. The integrated space within economic corridors relies upon free movements of labor and capital, and trade and investment flows. Successful corridors require economic density, as well as corridor-wide energy and transport linkages. Economic corridors can boost competitiveness enormously, through improved logistics, lowered costs of production of both goods and services, and enabling policies and investments for urbanization.

---

[14]   These include the Regional Comprehensive Economic Partnership and the Trans-Pacific Partnership, among others.

[15]   The *WTO Trade Facilitation Agreement*, which came into force in 2017, seeks to expedite the movement, release, and clearance of goods, including those in transit. It also sets out measures for effective cooperation between customs and other authorities, and enhances technical assistance and capacity building. The Trade Facilitation Agreement was ratified by all eight CAREC countries that are WTO members: Afghanistan, PRC, Georgia, Kazakhstan, the Kyrgyz Republic, Mongolia, Pakistan, and Tajikistan.

[16]   The International Convention on the Simplification and Harmonization of Customs Procedures (Kyoto Convention) of the World Customs Organization, came into force in 1974. It was amended to become the Revised Kyoto Convention in 2006, as the blueprint for modern and efficient customs procedures.

50. CAREC countries are urbanizing rapidly. Sustainable urbanization in the context of corridor development requires resilient infrastructure and connectivity, ties to a globalizing economy, human capital, and openness to trade in services, including tourism and higher education. In addition, border crossing conditions must be greatly eased. *CAREC 2030* can assist its members develop urban strategies from a regional corridor perspective through integrated linkages involving infrastructure—energy, road and rail, air, telecommunications—and knowledge and technology that will enable the production of both goods and services to move up the value chain. CAREC can also facilitate exchanges of services between the cities and surrounding regions—education, training, health, agriculture services, logistics, tourism, services linked to city planning, and environmental services. Finally, an important area for cooperation is disaster risk management. CAREC can serve as a platform for sharing knowledge among member countries in mainstreaming disaster risk management within urban planning.

51. The CAREC-supported *Almaty–Bishkek Economic Corridor* found strong resonance in the governments of the two countries and the two city administrations.[17] It has been designed to attract private investments, with emphasis on agribusiness, tourism, the digital economy, smart cities, health and education, and rapid intercity transport links. In the next phase, *CAREC 2030* will help further develop this corridor and assess the potential of other corridors in the region.

C. Infrastructure and Economic Connectivity Cluster

52. *CAREC 2030* will continue to advance the regional infrastructure agenda, in line with the SDGs' call for reliable and sustainable infrastructure, including regional and cross-border infrastructure.

53. CAREC will build on its strong record of investments in transport and energy, and support adoption of modern technologies for improved connectivity. Support will be extended to improve policy and governance frameworks, and mobilize funding from the public and private sectors. Attracting private sector finance will require improving the enabling environment for efficient leverage, risk mitigation, and securitization. *CAREC 2030* can also help bring the public and private sectors together to promote the development of effective public–private partnerships.

i. Transport

54. *Railways.* *CAREC 2030* will help build the potential of railways to become a leading carrier of freight and passenger traffic in the region. This will require operationalizing railway corridors by ensuring interoperability in conditions of three different rail gauge systems used in CAREC countries. In addition, international freight movements can be eased if regulations on freight logistics companies were liberalized. Finally, the establishment of a CAREC regional common rail operator serving as a single point of contact will be explored.

55. *CAREC 2030* will promote investments along the designated railway corridors to expand networks; improve rolling stock; and modernize technologies, signals, fiber optics, and electrification. Commercialization of national railway operators and increased private sector investment in railways will be facilitated by creating an enabling environment and improving competitive conditions, creating robust management and commercial capabilities, and modernizing regulatory frameworks. CAREC will be an important platform for investment planning and for promoting best-practice operating conditions and associated regulations.

56. *Aviation.* Stronger air connectivity among CAREC countries will add tremendous value for businesses and tourism development, and exports of high-value consumer goods. However, the lack of comprehensive aviation agreements

Support for railways, aviation and logistics infrastructure are key elements of CAREC's transport connectivity strategy

---

17 ADB. October 2016. *Almaty–Bishkek Economic Corridor: Investment Framework*. Manila.

among countries in the region is a current major constraint. Other limiting factors are lack of institutional capacity, tough challenges to air safety in harsh climates, and financial constraints for aviation infrastructure development. In all these areas, *CAREC 2030* can play a facilitating role.

57. CAREC will explore fostering aviation agreements, including open skies, and building knowledge and capacity consistent with international standards. Aviation agreements will drive a surge in traffic, not least by encouraging low-cost carriers, code sharing, and joint ventures; and generate resources for infrastructure and human capital development. A notable example is provided by the Association of Southeast Asian Nations single aviation market with its incremental implementation of liberalization over a decade that led to a strong growth in traffic, rise in exports, among others, by greater low-cost carrier penetration. CAREC will also explore the possibilities and potential of regional collaboration on aviation through in-depth analyses, regional stakeholder consultations, and capacity development activities.

58. *Road Transport. CAREC 2030* will continue to assist in completing road corridor investments, paying more attention to sustainability of road infrastructure. There will be an increased focus on road safety and road asset management. Institutional and financial reforms in the road transport sector will help improve road maintenance practices and enhance road asset life cycles.

59. Regional cross-border transport will continue under CAREC with an aim to reduce transport and trade costs. *CAREC 2030* is also well tooled to support the implementation of the TIR Convention,[18] by strengthening partnerships among national governments, the International Road Transport Association, national transport associations, and development partners. Other cross-border transport facilitation mechanisms, such as the universal customs guarantee, cross-border transport agreements for commercial

Regional approaches to technology adoption will create scale economies to make clean energy investments viable

freight and passenger operations, and driver visa facilitation will remain priority tasks for CAREC.

60. *Logistics infrastructure. CAREC 2030* will support investments in logistics infrastructure along the CAREC corridors. Greater attention will be given to those investments that create economic clusters and corridors by combining trade, production, and logistic functionalities within one facility. One such endeavor is the envisaged Trans-Caspian Multimodal Transport Corridor. Another example of such an investment is the Khorgos land port on the border between PRC and Kazakhstan, where the respective governments set up a center of regional trade and economic cooperation that has, over time, attracted private sector investments in production, trade, services, logistics, and transport. The creation of other similar land ports could be explored. Development of such investment projects will require strong partnerships among the governments and private sector investors through innovative public–private partnership institutional and financial arrangements.

ii. Energy

61. *Clean energy. CAREC 2030* will support technology leapfrogging in the use of clean and renewable energy to help curb carbon emissions to support sustainability and reduce carbon footprints of member countries. The emergence of new energy technologies together with the sharp drop in the cost of renewable energy generation are helping countries deliver on national commitments under climate change agreements, but require the integration of new options into national energy policies and into regional trade arrangements. CAREC's value addition will be on promoting cross-country learning and introducing regional approaches to technology adoption to help create economies of scale to make investments in clean energy viable. Such investments have the potential to add greatly to the current electricity generating capacity in the region. In addition to investments,

18 The Convention on International Transport of Goods or *Transports Internationaux Routiers*, establishes an international customs transit system with facility to move goods in sealed vehicles or containers from a customs office of departure in one country to a customs office of destination in another country, without requiring extensive and time-consuming border checks at intermediate borders while, at the same time, providing customs authorities with the required security and guarantees.

CAREC 2030 will provide research and advice on the clean and renewable energy agenda, including on building enabling policy and regulatory environments to attract private sector investments.

62. *Energy efficiency.* CAREC countries in Central Asia generally have high energy intensities, requiring attention to improving energy efficiency to support national competitiveness and address climate mitigation needs through reduced greenhouse gas emissions. Besides investments, *CAREC 2030* will promote enabling policies for energy efficiency in the region, including pricing and tariff reforms and building codes and standards. *CAREC 2030* may also promote emission trading systems, in the context of promoting trade and developing unified markets in the region, while raising efficiency in energy use.

63. *Energy trade.* CAREC has assisted developing regional energy master plans, providing technical support to Afghanistan for connecting with the Central Asian grid, and financing the interconnection between Turkmenistan, Uzbekistan, Tajikistan, Afghanistan, and Pakistan. Moreover, the work on the Turkmenistan–Afghanistan–Pakistan power transmission interconnection project and the Turkmenistan–Afghanistan–Pakistan–India natural gas pipeline project is advancing. CAREC will continue to support these existing energy trade initiatives, while reinforcing further integration of energy markets.

D. Agriculture and Water Cluster

i.   Agriculture

64. To promote regional trade in agriculture, *CAREC 2030* will support alignment of SPS measures with international standards, build capacity on product quality and diversity, and improve shipment linkages. This will help member countries integrate into regional and global agricultural value chains.

65. Support will also be considered for transboundary animal disease control as it requires cross-border collaboration, including biotechnology information sharing, bio-safety

coordination, and the harmonization of veterinary measures. Given the potential in many areas for horticultural exports, the development of a CAREC food safety network and a common quality control system that involves the management of pesticides and improved food safety standards would broaden access to export markets.

66. Agricultural growth in the CAREC region is threatened by its vulnerability to climate change. Adaptation capacities in farming, crops, and technologies are low, as is farmers' access to information and technologies. In particular, there are gaps in the provision of weather data, its analysis, and predictive tools for farmers. *CAREC 2030* can support investment in hydromet services, and projects to establish, train, and share experiences among national and subnational hydromet bodies. Assistance for environmental conservation of bioresources by adopting cross-country ecosystem approaches can be also considered.

ii.   Water Management

67. Despite the obvious complexities of the water sector, there is record of cooperation in the region on data sharing, institutional development, and joint management of the Amu Darya and Syr Darya basins. *CAREC 2030* can help build on this record and use its strengths, including its honest broker role, to promote discussion and dialogue on water issues to chart the way forward. *CAREC 2030* can provide a platform to discuss water scarcity and water productivity issues as well as to eventually explore transboundary water resource management.

68. A careful identification of consensual entry points for CAREC in the water is the essential first step. Irrigation and efficient agriculture development, improved management of river flows to reduce flood risk, and addressing water contamination are some "early harvest" areas for potential CAREC support. Moreover, assistance could also be provided in basin water management, particularly in transboundary areas. To promote water sector cooperation, CAREC can work in close partnership with the International Fund for the Aral Sea-associated institutions and international partners such

CAREC will help member countries integrate into global and regional agricultural value chains and promote cooperation in the water sector

as the World Bank Group and the United Nations Educational, Scientific and Cultural Organization's International Hydrological Programme.

E.   Human Development Cluster

i.   Education

69. CAREC countries have established networks of national and regional tertiary education and technical and vocational education and training institutions, consisting of universities, research institutes and think tanks, and vocational training schools. There are significant opportunities for regional trade in education services that expand supply and choice and enhance quality. The private sector can play an important role in this.

70. Collaboration can encompass instructional delivery initiatives such as student exchanges, development of branch campuses, and introduction of dual and joint degree or diploma programs, including e-learning programs. *CAREC 2030* can also support non-instructional initiatives such as faculty exchanges, research collaborations, cross-border accreditation, program and degree or diploma harmonization, mutual recognition of skills and qualifications, development of higher education and technical and vocational education and training institutions networks, and institutional twinning arrangements.

71. Promoting greater labor mobility to match employment opportunities in the region is important. *CAREC 2030* can help develop an integrated regional labor market information system focusing on providing information on current and future skill needs, and regional job search and placement services.

ii.   Health

72. Addressing pandemic risks and control of communicable diseases are critical regional public goods with significant positive externalities. *CAREC 2030* can support a common framework for addressing pandemics, given the likely regional nature of future outbreaks. The framework could include enhancing regional capacities to assess and respond to pandemic risks, and building preparedness to address regional health risks, including the development of early warning systems and regional surveillance centers.

73. There is also considerable room for making advances in the region for noncommunicable diseases. CAREC can facilitate common approaches and cross-learning in prevention and treatment protocols, help modernize service delivery and regulations, and develop sustainable financing models. CAREC can also facilitate private sector-driven trade in health services and e-medicine in the region.

Cross-border education services and control of communicable diseases will help improve quality of human capital

CAREC 2030: INSTITUTIONAL FRAMEWORK

VI

A.   A Renewed Institutional Framework

74. *CAREC 2030* will be implemented through a renewed institutional structure that promotes member countries' active and sustained participation in CAREC at both policy and project levels (see Figure). By providing an open platform for regional collaborative action, the renewed structure will enable and provide incentives to CAREC member countries and development partners to lead and facilitate initiatives in their respective areas of comparative advantage.

75. The renewed institutional framework is guided by the following elements:

- Building strong ownership and stakes of countries in CAREC at both senior and technical working levels;

- Enhancing the role of development partners, including capitalizing on their areas of expertise and resources to maximize their contribution to the expanded CAREC agenda;

- Establishing integrated groupings to activate cross-linkages between sectors, and create synergies;

- Introducing an incremental approach to building up implementation modalities in the new areas and fine-tuning these modalities over time based on progress;

- Retaining flexibility and pragmatism by allowing two or more CAREC countries to implement regional projects and initiatives agreed on by all members; and

- Strengthening engagement with the private sector and civil society at all levels.

76. The institutional arrangements for each of the five clusters will be defined based on the specific implementation requirements in each cluster. As a general approach, where clarity on the actual scope of work needs to be further developed, particularly in the new areas of operations (such as tourism, water, education, health, and others), a series of group discussions and workshops will be conducted. Such discussions could help develop a consensus on the key issues to be addressed, in what sequence, and the type of institutional structures that might be needed for successful implementation in the cluster or sector. Based on the outcomes of such discussions, expert groups in each area may be convened to kick off topical discussions, converge interest of member countries, identify concrete scope of activities and key issues of regional relevance, and conduct dialogue with key development partners (see para. 84). Ultimately, fully empowered sector committees, including necessary subworking groups, could be established as needed to develop and implement strategic action plans to move forward on the identified initiatives.

Figure: *CAREC 2030* Institutional Framework

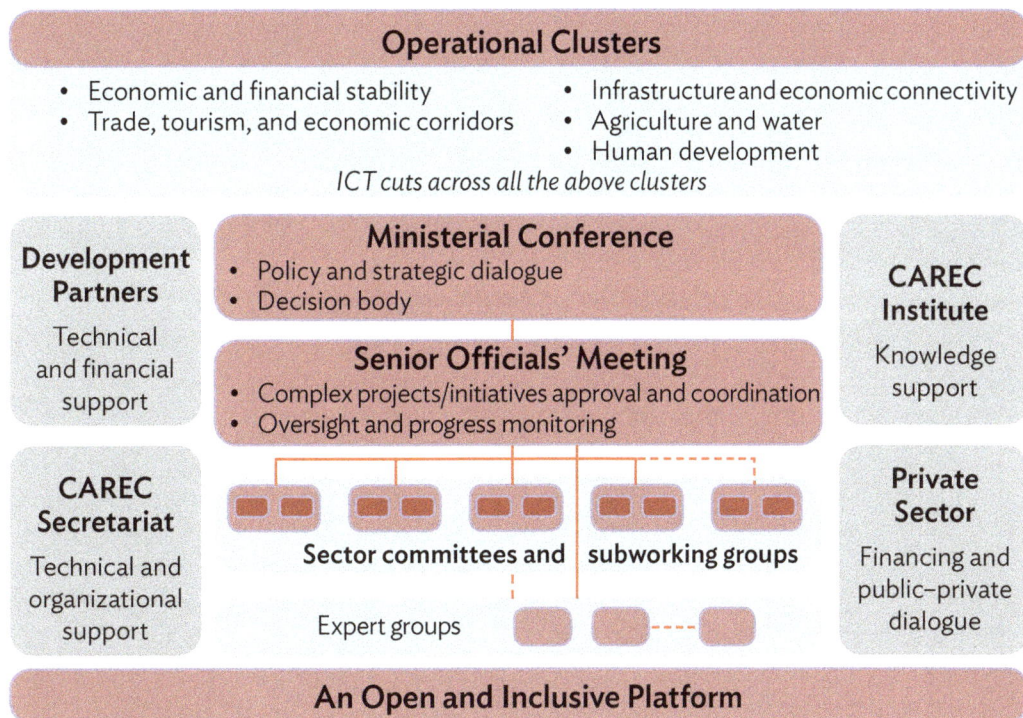

Operational Clusters

- Economic and financial stability
- Trade, tourism, and economic corridors
- Infrastructure and economic connectivity
- Agriculture and water
- Human development

ICT cuts across all the above clusters

Development Partners

Technical and financial support

Ministerial Conference
- Policy and strategic dialogue
- Decision body

Senior Officials' Meeting
- Complex projects/initiatives approval and coordination
- Oversight and progress monitoring

CAREC Institute

Knowledge support

CAREC Secretariat

Technical and organizational support

Sector committees and **subworking groups**

Expert groups

Private Sector

Financing and public–private dialogue

An Open and Inclusive Platform

CAREC = Central Asia Regional Economic Cooperation, ICT = information and communication technology.
Source: CAREC Secretariat.

B. Enhanced Role for the Ministerial Conference and the Senior Officials' Meeting

77. The MC will function as a high-level strategy-setting and policy body. It will serve as a platform to discuss and debate important policy and strategic issues of regional relevance, including measures to promote regional economic stability and macroeconomic policy linkages of CAREC operational sectors. It will also provide overall strategic guidance on issues of regional and supranational nature and advise on CAREC's external linkages with other regional cooperation bodies and multilateral institutions. The MC will exercise overall accountability over the results of the CAREC Program. Ministers will represent member countries at the MC, empowered with full decision-making rights, to help build high-level ownership and facilitate the achievement of results under the program.

78. A summit-level meeting of CAREC heads of states and/or governments may be considered on a periodic basis, every 3 to 5 years, to keep the political leadership informed and to reinforce high-level country ownership of the CAREC program. Such summit-level meetings could provide the opportunity for decision making on complex policy and coordination issues related to regional cooperation that require political consideration at the top levels of government.

79. With the MC focused on policy and strategy issues, the SOM will be empowered to monitor progress at the cluster and sector levels. The SOM could recommend operational improvements, and be vested with the authority to consider and endorse complex multi-country and multisector projects. The SOM will also serve as a mechanism to ensure the effective implementation of the policy and strategic decisions made at the MC level.

80. Given its enhanced responsibilities, it is crucial that senior officials from member countries with full authority who can decide on sector and project issues attend the SOMs. Ensuring continuity in representation of countries at the SOM is also important for its effective and uninterrupted functioning. National focal points will continue to play a critical role in ensuring high-level ownership of CAREC's operations in their respective governments, and in ensuring effective coordination between the governments and the CAREC Secretariat.

C. Sector Committees

81. An empowered SOM should not in any way diminish the critical roles and responsibilities of the existing or any new sector committees. Sector committees will continue to exercise full operational authority to discuss and develop options and recommendations for their respective sectors. They will also ensure effective and timely implementation of projects and initiatives under their area of competence. To further strengthen ownership of sector committees, member countries can consider becoming co-chairs of such committees together with interested development partners with expertise in relevant sectors. CAREC's existing sector committees will be adapted and streamlined to match the new cluster groupings. Subworking groups could be formulated under the sector committees who will report their work to these committees.

82. A trade committee will be created to discuss and deliberate on the increasingly intertwined issues of trade policy and trade facilitation in a synergistic manner. The composition of this committee will draw on officials and experts from relevant trade-related agencies in member countries. An immediate task of this committee will be to develop a trade strategy with forward-looking options and possibilities guided by the *CAREC 2030*. Customs cooperation functions related to trade facilitation will continue to be carried out by the standing Customs Cooperation Committee.

83. The existing Transport Sector Coordinating Committee and Energy Sector Coordinating Committee will continue to operate under the infrastructure and economic connectivity cluster. A subworking group on railways has been created for implementing the CAREC Railway Strategy 2030. Similarly, the Transport Sector Coordinating Committee may consider establishing an aviation subworking group as deemed necessary to deliberate on policy actions and investment projects in this subsector. The Energy Sector Coordinating Committee may, likewise, consider establishing subworking groups as needed.

D. Expert Groups

84. Given CAREC's evolving operational priorities, a flexible and demand-driven mechanism of expert groups could be constituted. Such task-based and issue-driven expert groups are needed to provide rapid responses to CAREC member countries' emerging priorities and changing needs. For example, expert groups on economic corridor development, tourism cooperation, or common skills and qualification standards in member countries may be considered after a series of group discussions to establish indicative directions in such areas. In addition, expert groups on cross-cutting issues such as ICT or climate change may also be constituted as needed. Such expert groups will be sharply focused and draw on the full range of expertise available from member countries and development partners.

E. Development Partners

85. The broadened scope of *CAREC 2030* provides new space for development partners to engage with the region in the five operational clusters for policy and capacity building support as well as investment projects. Development partners, both existing and new, could assume lead roles in the various areas, sectors, and subsectors based on their comparative advantages; and incubate new ideas and projects. Institutional procedures will be streamlined to facilitate development partners' membership and role in CAREC.

86. Development partners will be invited to co-chair SOMs on rotation to promote their

A flexible and demand-driven institutional set-up is important to strengthen the effectiveness of CAREC

active engagement in CAREC. In addition, a CAREC Development Partners' Forum could be convened from time to time to have a dialogue among development partners on strategic and operational matters related to the CAREC Program.

87. Development partners shall also be invited to second staff to the CAREC Secretariat on short-term and long-term assignments to support *CAREC 2030*. Greater transparency and enhanced information sharing among development partners will be ensured.

CAREC 2030 requires greater financial, technical and human resources to achieve tangible results

F. CAREC Secretariat

88. The CAREC Secretariat will continue to provide technical, administrative, and coordinating support for the implementation of *CAREC 2030*. The capacity of the Secretariat will be further strengthened to assist with the widened scope of CAREC's operations and activities going forward.

89. The role of the regional cooperation coordinators and the advisors to the national focal points based in member countries will be streamlined and improved. They will be tasked to provide effective on-the-ground support for the implementation of *CAREC 2030*. They will also be expected to raise visibility and awareness of CAREC by reaching out to national stakeholders, including think tanks, academia, civil society, and the private sector.

G. Private Sector

90. Mechanisms to promote private sector participation and investment, and foster public–private dialogue and interaction at CAREC forums will be promoted. Business and investment forums will continue to be convened to attract the private sector's attention and finances to support CAREC's projects and activities. Bilateral and regional business-to-business contacts will be encouraged.

91. The CAREC Federation of Carrier and Forwarder Associations, the first private sector mechanism established under CAREC to support transport and trade facilitation, will continue its activities and functions. Other similar initiatives of this nature could be considered to leverage the private sector's role in *CAREC 2030*.

H. Mobilization of Resources

92. With the expanded scope of *CAREC 2030*, greater financial, technical, and human resources will be indispensable to support and implement its key directions. ADB and other development partners will need to scale up their financial and technical support for CAREC's projects and activities. Joint efforts also need to be devoted to mobilize and generate more private sector interest and financing. Member countries may also consider more contributions to support and sustain the CAREC Program and its activities in the long run.

CAREC 2030: PROGRAM RESULTS FRAMEWORK

VII

93. The *CAREC 2030* program results framework demonstrates the results chain, leading from CAREC interventions to the expected outputs, and the targeted outcomes in each operational cluster that will contribute to the impact of "Sustainable economic development and shared prosperity in the CAREC region." (see Table) The results framework will help member countries and the CAREC Secretariat monitor progress on *CAREC 2030*.

94. No target indicators are provided at this stage in the results framework. The CAREC Secretariat will work closely with the sector committees and working groups to develop cluster and sector-specific results frameworks with concrete indicators, baseline data, and data sources at outcome and output levels. An online system of tracking and updating progress on these indicators with regular intervals will be established. The CAREC Secretariat staff will lead this work with active inputs from sector committees and working groups. Every 3 years, the CAREC Secretariat will prepare a consolidated progress report by taking stock of progress on the program results framework and cluster and sector level indicators supporting the framework. Progress reports will also be made available online.

Table: *CAREC 2030* Program Results Framework

Impact	Sustainable economic development and shared prosperity for the CAREC region				
	Economic and Financial Stability	**Trade, Tourism, and Economic Corridors**	**Infrastructure and Economic Connectivity**	**Agriculture and Water**	**Human Development**
Outcomes	Increased regional macroeconomic stability, improved investment, and financial integration	Expanded trade, competitive economic corridors, and tourism opportunities	Enhanced economic connectivity, and increased sustainability and resilience of regional infrastructure	Expanded agricultural trade, and effective transboundary water resource management	Increased regional cooperation in education and health
Outputs	Regular policy dialogue on economic stability issues institutionalized A forum of regulators activated to exchange information and experience on financial stability and associated issues Improved investment climate enabled	National single windows with improved border crossing points in place Economic corridors successfully developed Tourism services and infrastructure improved	Reliable, resilient and sustainable transportation systems operational Efficient use of energy increased	Regional and global agricultural value chains promoted Improved management of river flows and basin water management	Pandemic and noncommunicable diseases controlled Students and labor mobility increased to match employment opportunities
CAREC Interventions	Design and implement counter-cyclical policy responses as appropriate Promote cross-country coordination and adopt relevant financing models Reduce investor transaction costs, improve investment policies and regulations, and promote business for SMEs Support policies that increase cross-border financial integration and promote capital flow Exchange data and intelligence, and develop common practices to international standards	Scale up CAREC advance transit system and extend common information exchange across customs covering all trade and transit transactions Support post WTO-accession commitments Improve logistics and cost of production, and promote regional and global value chains in economic corridors Jointly develop tourism products and advocate harmonization of visa regimes	Establish multimodal transport network, cross-border railway infrastructure and services, and strengthen air connectivity while also investing in dry and land ports Bridge the gap between energy supply and demand by facilitating cross-border energy trade Promote energy efficiency and use of clean energy technologies	Align sanitary and phytosanitary standards; and build capacity on product quality, diversity, and finance agriculture infrastructure Invest in hydromet services. Adopt cross-country ecosystem approaches for environmental conservation of bioresources Employ international best practices in water management and transboundary water resource management	Develop an integrated regional labor market information system Promote mutual recognition of qualifications and quality assurance Set up health-related surveillance systems for pandemic communicable diseases Promote trade in health services and e-medication in the region
Driving Principles	Aligning with national strategies and supporting SDGs and COP21	Expanding operational priorities selectively	Deepening policy dialogue based on CAREC's standing and ability to deliver quality knowledge services	Integrating the role of the private sector and civil society	Building an open, inclusive CAREC platform

Source: CAREC Secretariat.

CAREC

CENTRAL ASIA REGIONAL ECONOMIC COOPERATION PROGRAM

TIMELINE 1996–2017

Technical assistance to promote **regional economic cooperation** in Central Asia is approved

Tajikistan joins CAREC

In 2001, six CAREC-related projects were approved with a combined value of $247 million

First **CAREC Senior Officials' Meeting** is held in Manila, attended by delegations from Azerbaijan, the PRC, Kazakhstan, the Kyrgyz Republic, Tajikistan, and Uzbekistan

Six multilateral institutions comm to the program

Azerbaijan a Mongolia joi CAREC

1996   1998   2001   2003

1997   2000   2002

Regional technical assistance for Central Asia supports projects that increase trade and cooperation between Xinjiang Uygur Autonomous Region of the **People's Republic of China (PRC), Kazakhstan, the Kyrgyz Republic, and Uzbekistan**

The **CAREC Secretariat** is established at the Asian Development Bank

First **Ministerial Conference** reaches consensus for a flexible, practical approach within a results-oriented institutional framework

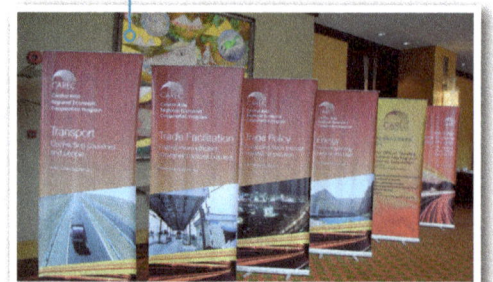

Afghanistan joins CAREC

The Energy Sector Coordinating Committee is formed

Ministers endorse the Transport and Trade Facilitation Strategy

The CAREC Institute Prospectus creates a mechanism to address "second-tier" issues of communicable disease control, environmental protection, business development, capacity–building initiatives, and research

Ministers endorse the Energy Action Plan Framework and CAREC's results focus

Private companies establish the CAREC Federation of Carrier and Forwarding Associations and start sharing cross-border movement data as the CAREC Corridors Performance Measurement and Monitoring Program is launched

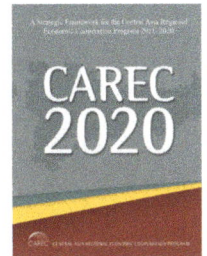

Ministers endorse the CAREC 2020, the strategic framework for expanding trade and improving global competitiveness

2005   2007   2009   2011

2004   2006   2008   2010

Transport and trade policy

coordinating committees are established. The private sector is encouraged to take part in the program

Comprehensive Action Plan

The First Business Development Forum sees business leaders and policy makers find ways to reduce impediments to regional cooperation

Inner Mongolia Autonomous Region of the PRC is brought into the partnership

The Trade Policy Strategic Action Plan is endorsed to help liberalize trade regimes and get member countries into the WTO

The Strategy for Regional Cooperation in the Energy Sector breaks ground as the first energy plan among Central Asian nations

Pakistan and Turkmenistan join CAREC

The Development Effectiveness Review is launched to monitor CAREC's performance process

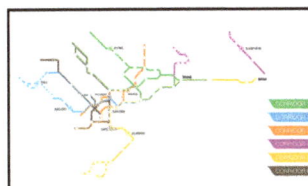

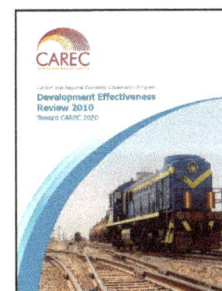

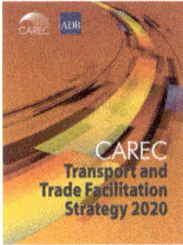

Ministers approve a refined strategy for transport and trade facilitation to integrate multimodal transport, improved logistics, more links to gateway ports, and better services at border crossings

Action plan for transport and trade facilitation comprises 108 investment projects worth $38.8 billion

Ministers approve Trade Policy Strategic Action Plan 2013–2017

CAREC Institute's physical base is launched in Urumqi, Xinjiang Uygur Autonomous Region, PRC

Georgia participates as an observer in the 14th Ministerial Conference

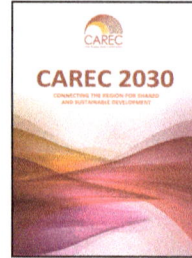

As of end September 2017, $30.5 billion in investments have gone into 182 CAREC-related projects

Ministers endorse CAREC 2030, a new framework to guide CAREC to better connect people, policies and projects as an open and inclusive platform

CAREC Institute obtains its legal status

2013

2015

2017

2012

2014

2016

58 projects worth $23 billion are prioritized to complete the six CAREC transport corridors

CAREC partners set a practical, results-oriented, and corridor-based approach to cross-border transport

Kazakhstan and the Kyrgyz Republic sign the Almaty–Bishkek Corridor Initiative to kickstart CAREC's economic corridor development drive

Transport Sector Workplan 2014–2016 is formulated with country- and sub-region-specific targets

Georgia becomes the 11th member of CAREC

Ministers endorse Mid-Term Review of CAREC 2020, Railway Strategy 2017–2030, and Regional Road Safety Strategy 2017–2030